Dive into Scripture!

Pursuing Spiritual Growth While Pressed by Difficulty

LYNN WISE

MW01234518

Dive into Scripture!: Pursuing Spiritual Growth While Pressed by Difficulty

Copyright © 2019 by Lynn Wise. All rights reserved. No portion of this book may be reproduced, stored in a retrieval system, or transmitted in any form or by any means, except for brief quotations in printed reviews, without prior permission from the author. Requests may be submitted by email: lynnwise609@gmail.com.

ISBN 978-0-578-58611-3

Unless otherwise noted, Scripture quotations are taken from the New King James Version. Copyright © 1982 by Thomas Nelson, Inc. Used by permission. All rights reserved.

Scripture quotations marked (NLT) are taken from the Holy Bible, New Living Translation, copyright © 1996. Used by permission of Tyndale House Publishers, Inc., Wheaton, IL 60189 USA. All rights reserved.

Scripture quotations marked (HCSB) are taken from the Holman Christian Standard Bible®, Copyright © 1999, 2000, 2002, 2003, 2009 by Holman Bible Publishers. Used by permission. Holman Christian Standard Bible®, Holman CSB®, and HCSB® are federally registered trademarks of Holman Bible Publishers.

Editing, cover design, and page formatting by ChristianEditingServices.com.

Blessed be the God and Father of our Lord Jesus Christ,
who has blessed us with every spiritual blessing
in the heavenly places in Christ.
—EPHESIANS 1:3

It is such an honor and blessing to study God's Word. Without His first teaching me, I would have absolutely nothing to say. Therefore, I dedicate this study back to God. My prayer is that the words that follow bring Him glory and honor as they draw us closer to Him. Praise Him!

I would also like to dedicate this study to my grandchildren, Fisher and Olivia Hart. They bring joy to my life and inspire me to finish well. It is my prayer that my life will honor Christ and point Fisher and Olivia Hart to Him. I love them so dearly and want to see them grow to know and love the Lord.

Contents

Preface

Life is a spectacular journey that allows us many exciting and challenging experiences. Some things are expected, and some come as a complete and utter shock. Some bring us great joy, and some bring us agonizing pain. Our experiences in life can and do take us through a full range of emotions. Stephen Covey said, "I am not a product of my circumstances. I am a product of my decisions."[1]

Life will happen. That is a certainty. But we have a choice to make. Will we react or will we respond? We can let our circumstances control us, or we can allow that which is within us to impact our circumstances. In the book of Genesis, Joseph chose the latter.

In the pages ahead, we will travel with Joseph on a lengthy journey. The journey has several unexpected twists and turns, yet Joseph chose to "dive in" to a deeper relationship with God and finish well. We will learn some valuable lessons as we follow his footsteps to fulfill his ultimate purpose in the history of Israel. These lessons will help us on our journey toward the purpose God has for each one of us.

I urge you to dive into Scripture and fully experience this journey. As we make stops along the way with Joseph, allow God to speak to you. Allow Him to show you how Joseph's example can impact your journey and subsequently allow you to impact others.

We have much to cover and much to learn. I am so glad you chose to dive into Scripture with me! My prayer is that through the pages that follow, God speaks specifically to you as He guides you on your unique journey to fulfill His purpose in your life.

Blessings,

Lynn Wise

Don't Panic, Submerge

 ## Daily Drop

Let me hear of your unfailing love each morning, for I am trusting you.
Show me where to walk, for I give myself to you.

— PSALM 143:8 NLT

As with most grandparents, I suspect, a night at BumBum's often includes a trip to Walmart. While my granddaughter carefully peruses all things pink and glittery, my grandson goes straight for the building-block sets. The higher the piece count, the greater the excitement. When we get home with a new set in tow, he rips into the box, grabs the instructions, and submerges himself into the imaginative world of plastic brick construction. With much care, patience, and concentration he searches out the right pieces and carefully puts them into place one by one. He doesn't come up for air until the masterpiece in his hands looks exactly like the one pictured on the box. He could make many things with all those little pieces. But to make them what they were intended to be, he knows the secret to success is found in the instructions.

Life can sometimes feel like a box of toy bricks. Circumstances often come with a high piece count. Difficulty and trouble can press in on us until we are unsure what to do. How can we ever become the masterpiece God intends us to be if we are constantly struggling to fit the pieces together?

What difficulties are pressing in on you today?

As in building that masterpiece with toy bricks, the secret to our success is found in the instructions. In 2 Timothy 3:12, Paul tells young Timothy that all who desire to live godly lives will suffer trials. Paul continues by describing the inspired Word of God much like a set of instructions leading us to spiritual success:

> **All Scripture is inspired by God and is useful to teach us what is true and to make us realize what is wrong in our lives. It corrects us when we are wrong and teaches us to do what is right.**
>
> — 2 TIMOTHY 3:16 NLT

But Scripture is so much more than a rule book. It is full of God's promises to His people. Psalm 46:1 tells us God's Word gives us refuge and strength. It is a very present help when we are experiencing trouble. Psalm 91:4 says we will find refuge under His wings. His truth will be our shield.

Which of God's promises do you cling to in times of trouble?

As we submerge ourselves in Scripture, God will show us we are not alone in our struggles. The pages of Scripture are filled with stories of God's people facing challenges. We find comfort as we see God's mighty hand at work in their lives amid difficult circumstances. He is at work in our circumstances as well. Mark Batterson gives this insight:

> God is in the résumé-building business. He is always using past experiences to prepare us for future opportunities. But those God-given opportunities often come disguised as man-eating lions. And how we react when we encounter those lions will determine our destiny. We can cower in fear and run away from our greatest challenges. Or we can chase our God-ordained destiny by seizing the God-ordained opportunity.[1]

Joseph, the favored son of the patriarch Jacob, encountered a lion of an opportunity. His intriguing story spans the last twenty chapters of Genesis. And a psalmist gives us a summary glimpse of God's hand at work as the pieces of Joseph's life come together:

> He called for a famine on the land of Canaan, cutting off its food supply. Then he sent someone to Egypt ahead of them—Joseph, who was sold as a slave. They bruised his feet with fetters and placed his neck in an iron collar. Until the time came to fulfill his dreams, the LORD tested Joseph's character.
>
> — PSALM 105:16–19 NLT

God was in control of this entire journey. God orchestrated the famine in the land—it was not by happenstance or coincidence. The famine was God ordained to set up the circumstances of Joseph's destiny. God allows and ordains our circumstances as well. They are all part of His master plan.

Prior to the devastating famine, God himself sent Joseph to Egypt. He was not sent as a diplomat or a prophet. Joseph was sent as a slave boy. He was placed precisely where he needed to be in order to grow as God intended him to grow. God allows our circumstances and our positioning for a reason.

What position has God put you in today?

There are many reasons for God's positioning. Here are a few. Which have you experienced?

Testing	**Healing**
Preparing	**Protection**
Pruning	**Growing**
Other_____	

God tested Joseph's character to prepare him to fulfill his dreams and God's plan for his life. Joseph passed with flying colors by submerging himself in his faith in God.

God tests our character as well, until the time comes for us to fulfill our destiny. Don't panic! Tests are intended to be passed, and this is an open-book test! All the answers are right there waiting for us to discover them in the pages of God's Holy Word. Our opportunities await.

Are you ready to submerge into God's wonderful Word? Breathe in God's goodness, grab His truths, and let's dive into Scripture together!

 ## Splash of Prayer

Ask the Lord to show you the growth opportunities He is placing before you.

The Pursuit of Spiritual Growth

 ## Daily Drop

For as the body without the spirit is dead, so faith without works is dead also.
—JAMES 2:26

Growth is an amazing process. We are born as helpless babies, and then immediately growth kicks in. Parents marvel at the differences one week to the next. But as time passes, we start measuring age in months and then years. The older we get, it seems, the more physical growth slows down, and then one day growth subsides and we are adults. Children are not only meant to grow; they are also expected to. If I stopped seeing physical growth in my grandchildren, I would quickly become concerned and urge my daughter to take them to the doctor.

God's Word tells us that when we become Christians, we become children, but in a different sense. Even if we are no longer physical children, we remain spiritual children. We are the children of God.

> **But to all who believed him and accepted him, he gave the right to become children of God. They are reborn—not with a physical birth resulting from human passion or plan, but a birth that comes from God.**
>
> — JOHN 1:12–13 NLT

As spiritual children, we are expected, even commanded, to grow. Let's review a few verses that explain our spiritual growth potential.

> I have not stopped thanking God for you. I pray for you constantly, asking God, the glorious Father of our Lord Jesus Christ, to give you spiritual wisdom and insight so that you might grow in your knowledge of God.
>
> — EPHESIANS 1:16–17 NLT

> I pray that your love will overflow more and more, and that you will keep on growing in knowledge and understanding.
>
> — PHILIPPIANS 1:9 NLT

> May God give you more and more grace and peace as you grow in your knowledge of God and Jesus our Lord.
>
> — 2 PETER 1:2 NLT

According to these verses, in what ways can or must we grow?

As children of God, we never reach spiritual adulthood here on this earth. Spiritual growth is a process, not an event. In fact, spiritual growth should be a never-ending process. Growth is not only learning. Our heads can be filled with volumes of spiritual knowledge, and yet we may experience no true spiritual growth. Spiritual growth must have a physical aspect as well.

How do you define spiritual growth?

Spiritual growth, in my simple definition, is continuously learning about God, believing what I learn, and then allowing what I know to be evident in my everyday actions. Simply put, it is ever-increasing Christlikeness.

Have you ever run into someone you haven't seen in a while? Eventually the conversation turns toward memories of the past. If you are like me, sometimes you may feel the need to clarify, to say, "I'm not the same person I was back then."

How are you measuring your spiritual growth? How far in the past do you have to go in order to say you are not the same person you were then? Ten years? Five years? One year? Six months? One month? Days?

No matter your comfort level with your answer to that question, you are in the right place. Diving into Scripture together is a perfect way to stimulate spiritual growth. We want to learn about God, then apply what we have learned. Repeated application through our works enables us to grow spiritually. Every day we want to grow a little more Christlike than we were the day before. Growth is mandatory if we want to fulfill our God-ordained destiny.

God revealed Joseph's destiny to him in a set of dreams, but Joseph had a lot of growing to do before he could fulfill that destiny. Let's take our first good look at young Joseph.

Read Genesis 37:1–10. How was Joseph favored?

What were his dreams?

Now read Genesis 42:1–10. How were Joseph's dreams fulfilled?

Now, here is the question that will take us the rest of this book to answer: What happened in the chapters between? In two words, spiritual growth. We see Joseph grow from a seventeen-year-old favored son into a strong, wise, God-honoring thirty-year-old man with whom God entrusted the fate of Egypt and the nation of Israel.

We learned from Psalm 105 in Lesson 1 that during this time of growth, God tested Joseph. God sent him to Egypt. God allowed him to be sold into slavery. In the face of all this hardship, Joseph chose to remain faithful. Joseph chose to trust God. He grew spiritually each time he passed a test placed before him.

Do you feel there is a test before you today? How will you grow spiritually as you choose to trust God, take Christlike action, and pass that test?

Whether you are just beginning your journey, finishing strong, or somewhere in the middle, you always have room to grow spiritually as you serve God. I am so excited to grow alongside you!

 ## Splash of Prayer

Ask God to strengthen your desire to pursue spiritual growth.

The Faith of our Fathers

Daily Drop

Abraham begot Isaac, Isaac begot Jacob, and Jacob begot Judah and his brothers.

— MATTHEW 1:2

There is a lot of enthusiasm these days about genealogy. I remember the big, four-inch thick family Bible displayed proudly on my parents' coffee table when I was a child. It was white with gold letters and sat in a wooden stand that allowed it to be closed or open. Written in the front of that old Bible was all the ancestry known to us. I remember tracing the tree with my finger and reading the names, some familiar and some not, until I got down to mine. This is my lineage. This is my family.

Joseph didn't have a family Bible on the coffee table, but he surely had something, maybe a scroll, that recorded the generations. The trunk of the tree had names like Abraham, Isaac, and Joseph's father, Jacob, whom God renamed Israel. Ten brothers were listed before him, one after. This was his family. The family that was, at that moment in Genesis, not so pleased with him.

Please read Genesis 37:10–11.

Joseph had now shared a second dream with his family. They were all pretty angry at him for thinking he would rule over them. But then something very interesting is recorded: Jacob "wondered what the dreams meant" (Genesis 37:11 NLT). I wonder if he put his hand on his hip as he paced back and forth with a limp. Joseph's forefathers were no strangers to messages from God. Was Jacob wondering, even hoping, that this was Joseph's turn to hear from God?

I am certain Joseph and his brothers had heard the story many times about how their great- grandfather Abraham had been directed by God to leave his home and go to an undisclosed location to live by faith. God had promised him an inheritance of that very land, and He promised that Abraham's descendants would be innumerable. Jacob's sons would have heard the story of how their great-grandmother had given birth to the son God had promised her in her old age. That son was their grandfather, Isaac. And of course, there was the story of how God directed Great-Grandpa Abraham to take Grandpa Isaac up on a mountain to offer him as a sacrifice. I am sure they were on the edge of their seats as Jacob told them how God had provided a ram at the last minute. Great-Grandpa Abraham hadn't wavered, because he had believed that if he sacrificed Isaac, God could raise him up from the dead.

The sons of Jacob had great faith because they had been taught about their faithful God. They learned from the great faith of their forefathers. How do I, today, know these stories were told? Because they were recorded for you and me in Scripture.

Please read Hebrews 11:8–9. Hundreds of years later, there is the record of Abraham's faith.

Please read Hebrews 11:11–12. Hundreds of years later, there is the record of Sarah's faith.

Please read Hebrews 11:17–20. There is the record of Abraham's faith, again. And then the record of Isaac blessing his two sons, Jacob and Esau.

Joseph knew this legacy of faith well, and I am confident he had faith in the same faithful God. So when he had a dream, both Joseph and Jacob had every right to believe it was from God and ponder the meaning.

Does your family have a story of faith that has been passed down from generation to generation? Please share!

What new story of your faith can you pass down to your descendants?

Please read Genesis 37:12–17. Where did Jacob send Joseph? Why?

Scripture tells us only that Jacob sent Joseph to bring back a report regarding his older sons and the flocks. Did Jacob expect more? Was he thinking back to his own journey to meet his brother after their falling out? Was he expecting Joseph to encounter God on this journey?

Read Genesis 32:22–32. Describe Jacob's encounter with God.

Jacob's life did a one hundred eighty-degree turn after his encounter with God that night. Jacob went from a trickster cheating to get his older brother's birthright to Israel, meaning "God Prevails." God changed Jacob that night. God would change Joseph as well. Joseph's transformation, however, would take thirteen years. During that time, he would rely on God completely, because he knew the God of Abraham, Isaac, and Jacob. Joseph had a rich heritage of faith that he would continue to live.

We too can completely rely on the one true God of the Scriptures. Every time we dive into His Word, we get a fresh taste of His goodness and His promises to us as believers. Like Abraham, Isaac, and Jacob, we must share our faith with those around us. Doing so will both strengthen us and help prepare others for their own encounters with God.

We are just getting started with Joseph. I cannot wait to see what God will teach us next as we continue to dive into Scripture!

 ## Splash of Prayer

Ask God to put people in your path who need to hear your story of faith.

Catalysts of Growth

 ## Daily Drop

A friend loves at all times, And a brother is born for adversity.

— PROVERBS 17:17

I have two older brothers. Some say they spoiled me. They say they raised me since they are thirteen and fourteen years my senior. To me, my brothers were heroes. They were larger than life and would do anything for their beloved little sister. My sisters, on the other hand, tell a different story. The four of them were stairsteps, barely a year between them. My sisters tell horror stories of how my brothers terrorized them. Joseph, no doubt, had similar stories.

With such a large family, Joseph certainly had a lot of family dynamics at play. First, let's take a look at Joseph's relationship with his father.

Please read Genesis 37:14–17. Describe Joseph's actions.

Joseph was obedient to his father. When Jacob asked him to go, there is no record of argument or delay. Joseph went. The journey was long, and he didn't find his brothers when he arrived at Shechem. It would have been easy for him to go back home and simply report they were not there, but Joseph didn't do that. He inquired about his brothers and traveled on to Dothan, where he finally found them. Joseph loved and respected his father and therefore was obedient. He was determined to complete his assignment.

Love and respect will always lead to obedience. Obedience to our heavenly Father will always lead to spiritual growth.

How have you shown love and respect to God the Father through obedience? Please describe. How did that obedience lead to spiritual growth?

Now let's look at Joseph's relationship with his brothers. **Please read Genesis 37:18–20.**

Were Joseph's brothers really this angry over a dream? The dreams may have just been the final issue that brought them to the point of doing something drastic. We know that Jacob showed Joseph favoritism because he was Rachel's firstborn son. He never even intended to marry Leah; he was tricked. Rachel was always the love of his life. We know that Leah's firstborn, Reuben, gave up his firstborn rights when he sinned against his father with Bilhah. Some speculate that the tunic of many colors was Jacobs's way of naming Joseph as his new heir. Joseph was number eleven in line. All these brothers who were now plotting against him had been passed over in this selection. This would be solid motive to plot the death of Joseph.

Joseph's relationship with his brothers was strained to say the least. Strained relationships can provide much opportunity to seek God's guidance and experience spiritual growth. When we see Joseph thirteen years after this, we will see a very different interaction between these brothers resulting from years of Joseph's spiritual growth.

Have you experienced spiritual growth as a result of a strained relationship? Explain.

Finally, let's take a look at a surprising change of heart. **Please read Genesis 37:21–24.**

Reuben had a plan. We are unsure what caused his change of heart. It could have been love for his brother. It could have been love for his father. It could have been fear of getting caught. Or it could have been an unwillingness to have blood on his hands. Whatever the reason, Reuben saved Joseph's life. Rest assured, God had His hand on the situation. He was positioning Joseph to begin his journey toward his destiny.

The cistern Joseph was placed in was made to hold water, although it was currently dry. There was no way of escape. Joseph was trapped, alone, and probably cold, and it was getting dark. Ruben's actions, whatever his motivations, placed Joseph where he had nowhere to look but up. Up was exactly where God wanted Joseph's focus.

When we have nowhere to look but up, God has our full attention. When we admit we have no control over our situation, that's when God begins His mighty work in our lives. Spiritual growth is imminent.

Are you in a place where you can see no way out? Look up, child of God! The Father is reaching down for you. He has a divine plan waiting for you. Dive into His Word, and He will show you His mercies, His grace, and His direction for your life.

 ## Splash of Prayer

Pray for God to reveal circumstances in your life that will lead to spiritual growth.

Submerged in Faith

Daily Drop

But You, O LORD, are a shield for me, My glory and the One who lifts up my head.

— PSALM 3:3

If you have never read through the Bible beginning to end, I highly recommend it. It is a wonderful growing experience. I purchased *The Daily Walk Bible* many years ago for just that purpose, and I go back to that old Bible from time to time. It has proven to be a trusted resource over the years. It's comforting, like an old familiar friend. The January 15 devotion makes this statement of Joseph:

> **Thirteen years of Joseph's life were spent in obscurity in Egypt. But they were not wasted years. God in his infinite wisdom knew that the man who emerged in chapter 41 would be different from the man who submerged in chapter 37.[1]**

God allowed Joseph's journey to take some unexpected twists and turns in order to grow him into the man He needed him to be and put him in the right place at the right time to fulfill his destiny. Is it too farfetched to expect that God does the same with us?

At this point in the story, Joseph is far from the right place at the right time. Or so it seems. In the last lesson, we left Joseph in a pit, actually a dry cistern, awaiting Reuben's rescue. **Please read Genesis 37:25–30.**

We don't know where Reuben went, but he was obviously gone too long. The other brothers' lack of conscience allowed them to sit down and eat a meal. While they were eating, God caused a caravan of Ishmaelites to pass by on their way to Egypt. Judah decided they could make a profit from this and lobbied to sell Joseph. **Please read Genesis 37:31–36.**

In an effort to cover their sin, the brothers devised a plan to deceive their father. They told a lie they had to live with every day afterward. As a parent, this breaks my heart for Jacob. For many years, the brothers watched their father grieve the son he thought had been killed.

Fast forward many years. **Please read Genesis 50:15–21.**

Joseph's brothers, after all these years, remained afraid of the repercussions of their actions against Joseph. Now that their father was gone, would Joseph get even? What they didn't understand was that Joseph was now a very different man.

Here is Joseph's famous response:

> **"You planned evil against me; God planned it for good to bring about the present result – the survival of many people."**
>
> — GENESIS 50:20 HCSB

Wow! What an amazing statement! While Joseph acknowledged the fact that his brothers' actions had indeed been evil, he also gave God the glory for His plan. God planned it and God accomplished it. God was with Joseph through the entire journey. God never left Joseph's side, and He will never leave ours.

God has never left your side. How does that give you comfort in your present circumstance? How can it help you move forward?

Where his brothers felt hatred, Joseph saw the Father's love for the promised nation of Israel. Where his brothers felt blame, Joseph chose forgiveness. Where his brothers saw the bonds of slavery, Joseph saw the freedom to grow. Where his brothers saw darkness, Joseph saw opportunity to shine for God. Where his brothers saw hopelessness, Joseph submerged himself in his faith and fulfilled his destiny.

What does the world see today in your circumstance?
What do you see?

Whatever our difficulty, submerging ourselves in our faith and diving into Scripture is the right answer. Looking at our circumstances through the lens of the Holy Scripture will give us a fresh perspective every time. Whatever evil this sinful fallen world sends against you, God can use it for good. Trust God's plan and bring glory to Him. "If God is for us, who can be against us?" (Romans 8:31).

Splash of Prayer

Pray for God to reveal opportunities for you to encourage someone by sharing how submerging yourself in your faith has carried you through a struggle.

Embrace the Challenge

 **Daily Drop**

For we walk by faith, not by sight.

— 2 CORINTHIANS 5:7

At age seventeen, I graduated from a very small high school. With the grand total of forty-four graduating seniors, my class was at the time the largest on record at my school. Between my position on the basketball team and my mom working at school, everyone knew me, and I knew everyone. The transition to college was a culture shock. I knew no one. The school was ten times the size of my high school. I didn't know where to go. I didn't know what to do. I came very close to quitting the first week. But I hung in there, made some friends, and eventually adjusted.

Describe a time you felt overwhelmed by a change in your surroundings.

At age seventeen, Joseph had been sold into slavery. Although his family was large, he had no frame of reference for where he was headed. Take a look at the account of Joseph's arrival in Egypt.

> **When Joseph was taken to Egypt by the Ishmaelite traders, he was purchased by Potiphar, an Egyptian officer. Potiphar was captain of the guard for Pharaoh, the king of Egypt. The Lord was with Joseph, so he succeeded in everything he did as he served in the home of his Egyptian master.**
>
> —GENESIS 39:1–2 NLT

I imagine Joseph's eyes widening as the traders' caravan approached the capital city of Egypt. Joseph caught the attention of Potiphar, the captain of the palace guard. Potiphar's home was no doubt in or near the palace, for Pharaoh would have kept members of his personal staff close. What a culture shock it must have been for Joseph. In what seemed like the blink of an eye, he had gone from flocks and fields to palaces and royalty. Overnight, he had fallen from favored son to servant. Going home was not an option.

Joseph could have gone into full-on panic mode, but there is no record of that. In these first two verses we start to see characteristics that will sustain Joseph through his entire captivity.

First, notice that Potiphar chose Joseph. He purchased him because, for some reason, Joseph stood out to him. We don't know how many slaves were on display that day. We don't know the cost. But what we do know is Potiphar's station in life. Potiphar would not have purchased an angry, aggressive slave. He could not afford to have a risky volatile ruffian near Pharaoh. He would have picked a servant who exhibited a calm and obedient character.

I submit to you, there is only one thing that can make a scared teenage boy ripped from his comfortable life and thrown into slavery appear calm and obedient. That one thing is faith that the one true God would see him through his difficulty. Faith often doesn't eliminate our circumstances, but it does allow us to weather them.

Hold on to the pattern of wholesome teaching you learned from me—a pattern shaped by the faith and love that you have in Christ Jesus. 2 Timothy 1:13 NLT

Paul encouraged Timothy to live by faith, just as many years earlier, Joseph had. When faith falters, fear enters. We must dive into Scripture and stand strong in our faith in order to successfully progress through our circumstances.

How has your faith in Jesus helped you progress where you would otherwise have been unable to?

Second, notice that Genesis 39:2 says, "The Lord was with Joseph, so he succeeded" (NLT). Joseph knew the Lord was with him, and that gave him hope. Without the Lord, we have no hope.

> So be strong and courageous, all you who put your hope in the Lord!
>
> —PSALM 31:24 NLT

Joseph drew his strength and courage from his confidence in the Lord. We also should have a confident hope in our Lord that strengthens us and gives us the courage to be successful in our circumstances.

How have you, or can you, be strong and courageous because of your hope in the Lord? Explain.

Third, we see Joseph serving his Egyptian master. We will talk a lot more about how he served later on. For now, let's think a moment about why he served. Joseph loved the Lord, no doubt. His faith and hope were evidence of that love. The Lord loved Joseph. The Lord being with him was evidence of that love. Joseph served with love because of the Lord's love flowing through him.

Love has been perfected among us in this: that we may have boldness in the day of judgment; because as He is, so are we in this world. There is no fear in love; but perfect love casts out fear, because fear involves torment. But he who fears has not been made perfect in love. We love Him because He first loved us. 1 John 4:17–19

When we understand God's perfect love, we can trust Him and face our circumstances with no fear. We may not love our circumstances, but we love the God who walks beside us through those circumstances. Understanding how much God loves us, even though we are sinners, helps us extend that godly love to others.

Thinking of your present circumstances, identify someone you have, or should have, shown love to because God first loved you. Explain.

If these characteristics sound familiar, it's because they are.

> **And now abide faith, hope, love, these three; but the greatest of these is love.**
>
> —1 CORINTHIANS 13:13

Why is love the greatest?

> Though I speak with the tongues of men and of angels, but have not love,
> I have become sounding brass or a clanging cymbal.
>
> —1 CORINTHIANS 13:1

Without love, we are just annoying noise. But with the love of God, we can maintain a calm and obedient character in the midst of any circumstances.

Joseph is just getting started on this journey. There are many twists and turns ahead. We will see Joseph make the best of his circumstances as he walks through them with the Lord at his side. Faith, hope, and love will be his foundation as he moves toward his destiny.

 ## Splash of Prayer

Ask God to show you where you can apply faith, hope, and love to your current circumstance as you walk closely beside Him.

Serve with Sincerity

Daily Drop

Bondservants, obey in all things your masters according to the flesh, not with eye service, as men-pleasers, but in sincerity of heart, fearing God. And whatever you do, do it heartily, as to the Lord and not to men, knowing that from the Lord you will receive the reward of the inheritance; for you serve the Lord Christ.

—COLOSSIANS 3:22–24

When I was a child, my dad and mom often told me, "If it's worth doing, then it's worth doing right." Maybe you recognize that phrase or one of these from your childhood.

- "Do what is right, not what is easy."

- "If you don't have time to do it right, when will you have time to do it over?"

- "It takes less time to do it right than it does to explain why you did it wrong."

- "Do the right thing first, not last."

Our parents taught us a "do it right" code to live by. This code is solid, whether you are washing a car or closing a business deal. Whether you are making your bed or building a skyscraper, doing things right matters. It's biblical. God tells us to do everything to the best of our ability, as if we are doing it directly for Him. This is especially important during the rough spots in life.

What are the primary areas where you feel it's most important to "do things right"?

When we last saw Joseph, his brothers had sold him as a slave. His service to his owner was just beginning.

Read Genesis 39:1–6. What are some key words the Scripture uses to describe Joseph's service?

Joseph was quite the success at running Potiphar's affairs. His situation was not ideal. When he left his father in Canaan to find his brothers, the thought probably never entered his mind that a few short days later he would be stripped of his robe and enslaved in Egypt. Joseph unexpectedly found himself in some serious trouble, yet he found success.

Joseph had a choice to make, as do we when faced with a trial. I pray none of us will be sold into slavery, but we often encounter unexpected circumstances that are less than ideal. How do we find success in our struggles? Let's see if we can find some clues in Joseph's actions.

> The Lord was with Joseph, and he became a successful man, serving in the household of his Egyptian master.
>
> —GENESIS 39:2 HCSB

The Lord was with Joseph while he served his master. Joseph was not pouting around, with his lip stuck out, doing things halfway. Joseph was serving his earthly master, and God blessed his service. When we serve, in any capacity and in any station, to the best of our ability and "do what is right," God will bless it. In serving others well, we serve God well. Note that God's blessing did not remove Joseph from slavery, and He didn't make his path smooth, but the Lord was with him and made him successful in his efforts.

> When his master saw that the Lord was with him and that the Lord made everything he did successful, Joseph found favor in his master's sight and became his personal attendant. Potiphar also put him in charge of his household and placed all that he owned under his authority.
>
> —GENESIS 39:3-4 HCSB

There it is again. Did you catch it? The Lord made everything Joseph did successful. Joseph was doing, and God was blessing. So often when we hit a rough spot, we are tempted to sit and feel sorry for ourselves or put all our efforts toward a way to escape. That was not the case with Joseph. He was doing and being blessed for it. The entire household was blessed because of Joseph. Potiphar's crops and livestock flourished. Potiphar was the one who sat back on his heels. The only thing he had to worry about was the dinner menu. Read Genesis 39:5–6.

Describe a current circumstance in your life that is less than ideal.

Who and how well are you serving in that circumstance? Explain.

Who is being blessed by your doing?

Is there something more you can do that will please God and bring His blessing on the situation?

This is one of those lessons learned the hard way for me. If my doing is sincere, and no matter who I serve, I serve as if I'm doing it for the Lord, I am blessed. When we work for God's glory, our entire outlook dramatically changes. We can see blessings overflowing to those around us, even those kicked back on their heels. That's okay, because we are doing the right thing for the right reason. I will take that blessing any day of the week. How about you?

 ## Splash of Prayer

Pray that the Lord shows you where He wants to see more sincerity in your doing.

Maintain Your Integrity

Daily Drop

The Lord is more pleased when we do what is right and just than when we offer Him sacrifices.

—PROVERBS 21:3

We have all heard the phrase, "All is fair in love and war."[1] We use this quote most when we want to justify—let's just say it—sinful actions. It implies that anything goes, with no holds barred. But in a battle, there is an assigned place or station. There are required actions. There is a critical spiritual "battle station" known as integrity. Maintaining our integrity in any situation is of utmost importance. Maintaining integrity in a crisis allows us to better shine for Christ.

Things were not the best for Joseph in Egypt, but he was making the best of his circumstances. God was blessing him, and Potiphar had put Joseph in charge of all his affairs. Then things took a sharp downward turn. Joseph was thrown into an even worse crisis, and his integrity was put to the test.

Read Genesis 39:6–9.

The Message describes Joseph as a "strikingly handsome man." The Holman Christian Standard Bible describes him as "well-built and handsome." It seems Joseph was good looking, strong, and smart! He caught the ladies' attention, no doubt. Unfortunately, that didn't play out very well for him.

"Integrity is doing the right thing when you don't have to—when no one else is looking or will ever know—when there will be no congratulations or recognition for having done so."[2] That day in the palace, when no one was looking, we see two distinctly different actions. First, let's take a look at Potiphar's wife. I encourage you to read this in multiple translations.

> **After some time his master's wife looked longingly at Joseph and said, "Sleep with me."**
>
> —GENESIS 39:7 HCSB

What about this verse catches your attention?

Let's zoom in on one phrase: "After some time" implies that this wasn't a spur of the moment thing. Potiphar's wife apparently had too much time on her hands, and she filled that time with observing Joseph. There is absolutely no indication that Joseph did anything to encourage her. She "looked longingly" at Joseph. Infatuation takes dedicated idle time. The Proverbs 31 woman would have taken no part in this activity.

> **She watches over the ways of her household, and does not eat the bread of idleness.**
>
> —PROVERBS 31:27

"The devil finds work for idle hands."[3] And he certainly succeeded here. Idleness is the enemy of integrity. In times of crisis, we must stay focused and keep our eyes on Christ. If we allow our idleness to focus on sin, it is just a matter of time until we lose our integrity.

Reflect a moment on your daily activities. I'm sure at first glance any twenty-first century woman would say she has no idle time. And we absolutely have no unfilled time. We are the queens of scheduling and multitasking. Everyone, however, has discretionary time and a choice of how to spend it. Dr. Voddie Baucham makes a very convicting statement: "You say you don't have time, but you have an active Netflix account. You say your day is full, but your Facebook status is up to date."[4] Ouch! And I have heard the argument, "I look at Facebook when I am stopped at a red light." You know, I have also heard of Bible verses being taped to dashboards for that very occasion. Don't get me wrong, these other things are not bad things, but they are also not eternal things. So let's dare to get real with God today.

What "idle" activities can/should you trade for some alone time with God?

Now stay with me here, and let's take a quick look at Joseph's response. Joseph was far removed from anyone who was watching to see if he maintained his integrity. Yet he stood strong. Simply put by The Message, "He didn't do it." Joseph cites two very valid reasons he would not compromise:

- First, it would violate Potiphar's trust.

- Most importantly, it would be a sin against God.

Joseph knew what was right, and he did it. I am not sure who said it, but it is true: "Trust takes years to build, seconds to break, and forever to repair."[5] A person's trust is a valuable thing to have. It is a huge part of integrity. Without trust, how can we ever reach people for Christ? And trust is built by consistency.

Describe areas in your life where you would like to show a little more consistency in order to gain someone's trust. What actions will you take to gain that trust?

While Joseph's relationship with Potiphar was important, it was nothing compared with Joseph's relationship with God. He refused to willingly sin against God. That, my friend, is integrity, and it is vital when we are faced with a trial. If under pressure we cannot maintain integrity, then we will lose our witness altogether.

What sin is before you today that must be refused?

We must anticipate temptation. We must decide before the time comes what our action or inaction will be.

What is your plan to accomplish refusal?

Using our time well, being trustworthy, and refusing sin are all key building blocks for integrity. Joseph exhibited them well. This lesson is not meant to tear us down but to encourage and instruct us in how we can better shine for Christ. Friend, it is never too late to shine.

 ## Splash of Prayer

Pray that the Lord show you where He wants to see your integrity shine.

Avoid Temptation with Agility

 Daily Drop

Therefore we also, since we are surrounded by so great a cloud of witnesses, let us lay aside every weight, and the sin which so easily ensnares us, and let us run with endurance the race that is set before us, looking unto Jesus, the author and finisher of our faith, who for the joy that was set before Him endured the cross, despising the shame, and has sat down at the right hand of the throne of God.

—HEBREWS 12:1–2

"Run, Forrest! Run!"[1] said Jennie, as trouble came their way. Forrest Gump, at least as a child, is not the picture that comes to mind when you think of agility. After all, he had braces on his legs. But one day when he ran, the braces fell away, and he ran like the wind.

While a degree of agility is God-given, maximum agility is trained. The most agile running back practices and trains his God-given talent every day. When the time comes to zig or zag, he doesn't even have to think about it. His body automatically responds to the circumstances of the defender coming his way. To be spiritually agile also requires practice. If we desire to automatically respond biblically to the circumstances coming our way, we must be diligent to practice every day.

Read Genesis 39:10–18.

As we take a few moments to explore this passage, we will discover some components of being spiritually agile.

The encounter starts out with, "as she spoke to Joseph day by day . . . he did not heed her" (Genesis 39:10). Joseph encountered temptation every day when he walked into his workplace, yet he stood firm in his convictions. He said what he meant and meant what he said. He practiced faithfulness every day. He could not change his workplace, for Potiphar owned him, but he could uphold his beliefs and not allow his circumstances to compromise his principles.

Before you answer the following questions, I want to remind you that temptation takes on many forms. What tempted Joseph might not be your temptation. So think for a moment, what is your weakness? What tempts you to go against God's will? Then answer these questions.

Do you have a daily encounter with temptation? Explain.

Can you change your circumstance?

If you said yes, how and when will you do that?

If you cannot change your circumstance, how will you stand firm?

Now this particular day, when Joseph went to work, "none of the men of the house was inside" (Genesis 39:11). Red alert! This is not a drill! Battle stations! Oh my, this is not going to end well!

> Be sober, be vigilant; because your adversary the devil walks about like a roaring lion, seeking whom he may devour.
>
> —1 PETER 5:8

Stay alert, my friend! Joseph missed a huge, flashing warning. This was a time for the buddy system. Some may need a buddy for accountability. Some may need a buddy to witness the fact that nothing happened. Either way, there is safety in numbers. The roaring lion was upon Joseph and seeking to devour him.

In what ways are you staying alert to your surroundings, not allowing the devil to catch you off guard? Are there opportunities to improve? Describe.

Run, Joseph! Run! Joseph was swift to respond. He zigged when she zagged, and he left her in the dust, holding nothing but his garment. Facing a roaring lion demands swift, deliberate, and decisive action. Joseph was trained up and ready. He didn't think; he simply and swiftly removed himself from the danger.

Are you ready to take swift action? When left alone with your temptation, what is your plan?

Finally, Joseph left something behind. Potiphar's wife caught his garment while trying to force him into sin. So often we find ourselves "ensnared" with something that is hindering our escape—or worse, pulling us toward sin. Joseph was ensnared physically. Just as easily, we can be ensnared mentally or even spiritually. This is the second time we see Joseph stripped of a garment because of some else's impure motives. He did not tarry to see if he could salvage his shirt. He fled, instinctively running in the opposite way from sin.

Remember, being tempted is not a sin. Jesus was tempted, but He never sinned. Falling to temptation is where sin enters the picture.

Are you ensnared with something today that is holding you way too close to sin? Explain.

What is God asking you to leave behind in order to flee from the sin that so easily ensnares you?

Joseph was the personification of spiritual agility. He was faithful, staying true to what he knew to be right and good. He faltered just a little in being alert, but he made up for that with his swift and immediate response to temptation. Without a second thought, he quickly left behind the thing that was trapping him with sin.

Agility is a powerful skill that becomes mandatory when we face a tempting circumstance. As we wrap up, read back over your answers to the questions in this lesson. Consider those answers as you close in prayer.

 ## Splash of Prayer

Pray that the Lord help you strengthen your spiritual agility.

Persevere with Grit

Daily Drop

Dear brothers and sisters, when troubles of any kind come your way, consider it an opportunity for great joy. For you know that when your faith is tested, your endurance has a chance to grow. So let it grow, for when your endurance is fully developed, you will be perfect and complete, needing nothing.

—JAMES 1:2–4 NLT

Sometimes, as hard as we pray, we don't get an easy answer. We bathe circumstances in prayer, yet it seems those prayers go unheard. Despite our doing everything right, things go horribly wrong. Our faith is often tested. God doesn't test us without reason, though. Our trials are intended to produce endurance. Let endurance grow. What work is endurance doing? It is making us "perfect and complete, needing nothing." For what purpose are we lacking nothing? Endurance is preparing us for the purpose God has in store for us. Endurance fertilizes our spiritual growth so we can reach our potential for Christ.

Another word for endurance is grit. I love that word. Endurance sounds tiring, but grit has a sound of the determination I want to have. Grit requires passion. Grit is the strength needed—physical, mental, and spiritual—to get the thing done. Grit doesn't give up, and it doesn't give in. God wants children with grit.

Read Genesis 39:16–23.

Joseph had done everything right, yet his circumstance seemed to spiral downward. He was accused falsely, convicted on circumstantial evidence, and sentenced to indefinite incarceration in the king's prison. This could have been a story of complete despair, but it's not. Why? In a word, grit. Joseph had more maturing to do, and it required him to exercise his endurance.

What do you see in Joseph's prison experience that seems familiar?

This makes me want to sing, "Second verse, same as the first."[1] An element of endurance is consistency. We must stay the course. Joseph went about his "doing" as he persisted. He never broke stride.

Spiritual strengths are not of a "choose one or another" mentality. Some may say they are tools in a toolbox, but tools may or may not be used. I would rather describe spiritual strengths as plays in a playbook. Used consistently and at the right time, they can bring success.

Mark Batterson writes, "We mistakenly think of righteousness as doing nothing wrong, when, in fact, righteousness is doing something right."[2] Joseph didn't simply sit in prison. He built his spiritual grit by doing the right things. He was sincere in his work, as if working for the Lord. He maintained his integrity and remained completely agile, ready to do the right thing at a moment's notice. Don't miss that. Joseph looked for opportunities to do the right thing. And whatever he did, the Lord caused him to prosper.

We don't have to wait until we are in a crisis to do the right things, although that is an excellent place to exercise our spiritual grit.

Are you feeling a little held captive today? Explain.

What opportunities do you see for doing the right thing?

Let endurance fully develop in you so that you lack nothing. I am not brave enough to pray for endurance, since it is also translated as patience. But I will be brave enough to pray for some spiritual grit to be consistent in my walk. Consistency in doing the right thing glorifies God and brings us closer to that completeness in Him that lacks nothing.

On a scale of 1 to 10, what level of spiritual grit do you have today? Where do you want it to be? Explain.

Let's wrap this up with this powerful quote from Charles Spurgeon. (Where he says "men" I am inserting "and women," for we are called to the same stance.):

> I pray God to send a few men [and women] with what the Americans call "grit" in them; men [and women] who when they know a thing to be right, will not turn away, or turn aside, or stop; men [and women] who will persevere all the more because there are difficulties to meet or foes to encounter; who stand all the more true to their Master because they are opposed; who, the more they are thrust into the fire, the hotter they become; who, just like the bow, the further the string is drawn, the more powerfully will it send forth its arrows, and so, the more they are trodden upon, the more mighty will they become in the cause of truth against error. Resolve, brothers and sisters, when you are in any sort of persecution, to face it with a full countenance. Like a nettle is the persecutor; touch it gently and it will sting you, but grasp it, and it hurts you not. Lay hold of those who oppose you, not with rough vengeance, but with the strong grip of quiet decision, and you have won the day.[3]

 ## Splash of Prayer

Pray today that God would reveal to you opportunities to do the right thing even when it is the hard thing.

A Time to Trust

 ## Daily Drop

To everything there is a season, A time for every purpose under heaven.

—ECCLESIASTES 3:1

This has been a stressful season for me. There has been a lot of travel, tight deadlines, and short fuses. I have a colleague with similar challenges and we frequently, shall I say, compare notes. One day I was being very vocal about my "notes," and he said something to me that totally shook me. He said, "Lynn, you might as well face it. Your circumstances are not going to change. You have to figure out how you are going to deal with it."[1] Well, that just made me a little angry. Okay, a lot angry. But when I got over my pride, I realized he had made a profound point.

In the middle of my circumstance I have, as we all have, two choices:

1. We can allow our circumstances to come in and get us all messed up inside. This choice will negatively impact us and quite possibly those around us.

2. We can trust God and allow the Holy Spirit within us to come out. In the midst of our circumstances, we will be positively impacted, and we can positively impact those around us.

This revelation blew me away. I had been letting my circumstances dictate my feelings and actions, when I should have been trusting the Spirit to take control and help me show Christlikeness in my circumstances.

To say that Joseph's circumstances were stressful is an understatement. His life seemed to be spiraling out of control. With his latest transition from slave to prisoner, his circumstances appeared to be getting more and more desperate.

Before we dive headlong into the twists and turns of chapter 40 of Genesis, I want to spend some time, pun intended, bridging the gap. Let's revisit the end of chapter 39.

> So he took Joseph and threw him into the prison where the king's prisoners were held, and there he remained. But the LORD was with Joseph in the prison and showed him his faithful love. And the Lord made Joseph a favorite with the prison warden. Before long, the warden put Joseph in charge of all the other prisoners and over everything that happened in the prison. The warden had no more worries, because Joseph took care of everything. The Lord was with him and caused everything he did to succeed.
>
> —GENESIS 39:20–23 NLT

Potiphar had placed Joseph in the prison where the king's prisoners were held. This is important because this is another step in God's plan to move Joseph closer and closer to the realization of His plan. I included verse 20 today for the last three words: "there he remained." That phrase has some finality to it, doesn't it? Did Joseph hope to ever get out of prison? Did his situation seem hopeless to him?

Joseph was human, so I'm sure he had those days when he was discouraged. This season of Joseph's life was, however, a season built firmly on trust in the Lord. Verse 21 gives us this assurance: "But the Lord was with Joseph in the prison and showed him his faithful love." Doesn't that just warm your heart? Joseph never went without feeling the faithful love of the Father. Even though Joseph remained in prison, the Lord never left his side. God's faithful love allowed him to experience this season with complete trust in God's plan.

Have you ever been in a circumstance where "there she remained" could have been the end of the caption? How did God's faithful love allow you to trust in His plan?

Verse 22 brings us to our next snippet of time. "Before long" Joseph was in charge again. The Lord was showing his faithful love by working things in Joseph's favor. Even though Joseph remained in prison, he was quickly rewarded for continuing to serve well, just as he had with Potiphar. Joseph trusted the Lord and allowed the godly character within him to impact the situation around him. Just like Potiphar, the warden had no worries because everything was running smoothly thanks to Joseph's service. Joseph's trust in the Lord allowed him to stand the test of time.

When we find ourselves in an extended undesirable circumstance, we must put our faith and trust in God. He will show us His unfailing faithful love. And before long, we will see His hand at work in our lives as we allow the Spirit within us to impact the circumstances around us. We too can stand the test of time as we trust in God and submerge ourselves in His loving Word.

How can you allow the Spirit of God within you to impact the circumstances around you today?

I know that sounds difficult to put into practice, especially in the midst of a difficult circumstance. Let's take a little encouragement from Henry Ford: "When everything seems to be going against you, remember that the airplane takes off against the wind, not with it."[2]

Although facing the winds of difficulty head on may be daunting, it's that very resistance that gives us spiritual lift. Trust God, face the day, and sooner or later you will take flight.

 ## Splash of Prayer

Pray that the Lord reveals areas where trusting the Spirit within you can lead to His impacting the circumstances around you.

Choose Peace

Daily Drop

"I have told you all this so that you may have peace in me. Here on earth you will have many trials and sorrows. But take heart, because I have overcome the world."

—JOHN 16:33 NLT

Albert Einstein is credited with saying, "Peace cannot be kept by force; it can only be achieved by understanding."[1] In a similar fashion, we cannot force the peace of God into our lives. We achieve it by understanding more and more about Him. In John 16, Jesus is explaining to His disciples that He would be returning to His Father soon. In verse 33, He gives the disciples a profound lesson about peace by explaining that you may have peace, but you will have many trials and sorrows. Trials and sorrows are a certainty. Peace is a choice. Think about that for a moment.

How does that resonate in your heart?

As we begin Genesis 40, we find Joseph right where we left him, in prison. I want you to see this section in the New Living Translation.

> Some time later, Pharaoh's chief cup-bearer and chief baker offended their royal master. Pharaoh became angry with these two officials, and he put them in the prison where Joseph was, in the palace of the captain of the guard. They remained in prison for quite some time, and the captain of the guard assigned them to Joseph, who looked after them.
>
> —GENESIS 40:1–4 NLT

We are unsure how long Joseph had been in prison at this point, but it is now "some time later," and Joseph was getting new cellmates. Verse 4 tells us that after the two joined Joseph, "They remained in prison for quite some time." These two time-related qualifications within the span of four short verses lead us to believe that this stint in the king's prison was lengthy.

The only hint of Joseph's condition is the fact that he remained in charge of the prisoners. These new inmates were assigned to Joseph's care, and he looked after them. From all indications, it was business as usual for a long time.

Have you been, or are you now, in a situation where it seems nothing is changing? Explain.

A trusted friend once gave me this advice: "If God hasn't directed you to the next thing, keep doing the last thing He directed you to do."[2] We have seen Joseph serve well. Now we see no evidence that he has changed course. He is doing the last thing he was directed to do.

What is the last thing God directed you to do? Are you at peace continuing in that direction?

So how do we find peace during an unchanging circumstance? Paul best verbalizes the concept in his letter to the Philippians, where he wrote of the secret to peace in the midst of all circumstances.

> I don't say this out of need, for I have learned to be content in whatever circumstances I am. I know both how to have a little, and I know how to have a lot. In any and all circumstances I have learned the secret of being content, whether well fed or hungry, whether in abundance or in need. I am able to do all things through Him who strengthens me.
>
> —PHILIPPIANS 4:11–13 HCSB

Warren Wiersbe has this insight into contentment:

> Contentment is not complacency, nor is it a false peace based on ignorance. The complacent believer is unconcerned about others, while the contented Christian wants to share his blessings. Contentment is not escape from the battle, but rather an abiding peace and confidence in the midst of the battle.[3]

Paul displayed this peace by singing hymns and praising God while he and Silas sat in jail. The shared blessing? The jailer and his family were saved. John displayed this peace by writing the book of Revelation while he was on the Isle of Patmos. We all share the blessing of their writings.

How do you see Joseph displaying this definition of peace and contentment?

How about you? How are you displaying peace in your circumstance? Describe.

Does this seem difficult? How can we have peace in the middle of the battle, as Wiersbe suggests? Paul gives us that answer too. We just need to back up a few verses.

> Be anxious for nothing, but in everything by prayer and supplication, with thanksgiving, let your requests be made known to God; and the peace of God, which surpasses all understanding, will guard your hearts and minds through Christ Jesus.
>
> —PHILIPPIANS 4:6–8

Our peace in the battle is through none other than Christ Jesus. Isaiah 53:5 tells us, "The chastisement for our peace was upon Him, and by His stripes we are healed."

And 2 Chronicles 20 tells us that the battle is not even ours; it belongs to God. Jesus assures us He has overcome the world. That, my friend, gives me a great deal of peace in any circumstance.

 ## Splash of Prayer

Thank Jesus today that He has overcome the world. Turn your battle over to Him and choose His peace.

Acts of Kindness

 **Daily Drop**

Do to others as you would like them to do to you.

—LUKE 6:31 NLT

Imagine for a moment that you are in a long line at the grocery store, your cart overflowing, and you notice the person behind you has one item. What do you do? We would all like to say we would invite them to move in front of us in line. But what if you are running late? What if you have had a bad day? What if? What if? Simple acts of kindness are something we all want to do, but how often do we actually deliver?

In the scenario above, what if the roles were reversed? What if you were the one with one item in the long line? What would you want the person in front of you to do for you? That's really what Luke is inviting us to take the initiative to do, isn't it? He is asking us to put ourselves in the other person's shoes and act accordingly. Whatever is going on with me is irrelevant; what is relevant is how I can do the right thing for someone else. But to put someone else before ourselves is a totally foreign concept in today's world.

When we last saw Joseph, he had been assigned a couple of new prisoners. Pharaoh's chief cupbearer and chief baker had offended him, and he had thrown them in the same prison where Joseph was being held. You will recall that they had been there for quite some time. Take a look at how Joseph interacted with the two.

Read Genesis 40:4–7.

This is just the beginning of this portion of the story, but we need to pause and narrow our focus to how this interchange began. First, let's take a look at the circumstance of the cupbearer and the baker.

In verse 5, what had happened to the cupbearer and the baker?

In verse 6, what was their appearance like the next morning?

That's pretty simple, right? The two guys each had a dream, and it was still evident the next day that they were upset by them. They knew in their hearts that the dreams were not simply dreams. They were sure these dreams had meaning, but they didn't understand.

Enter Joseph.

Where does verse 4 remind us the three are?

What does verse 6 tell us Joseph did?

What does verse 7 tell us Joseph asked?

Life did not change for Joseph since the last time we checked; he remained in captivity. If we are not careful, prolonged exposure to an undesirable circumstance can affect our Christlikeness, but Joseph acted with kindness as he encountered these two in this divine appointment.

Before we dig into how Joseph showed kindness, I don't want to miss the fact that this was a divine appointment. The actions taken on that morning set in motion the domino effect that ultimately freed Joseph. It is important to stay alert and recognize the divine appointments God puts in our path. Look for them and expect them. Our spiritual progress depends on recognizing and acting on these divine appointments.

Looking back at verse 6 in the NKJV, the Word tells us Joseph "looked at them," and then he "saw" their emotional state. Do you agree that many people look, but few ever really see?

When have you needed someone to see your circumstance? Did they?

When have you looked past the superficial and really seen someone else's circumstance?

To be able to do unto others, you first must see the others' circumstances, their feelings, their needs. Think back to the grocery store line. You first have to notice the person behind you and then see they have only one item. Without that, you will never see the opportunity to take action.

Verse 7 shows Joseph taking the initiative to act, to show kindness, when "he asked" why they were sad. Peter Drucker says, "Plans are only good intentions unless they immediately degenerate into hard work."[1] Once we see the opportunity to take initiative, we must act. We must act. Shall I say that again? We must act. We can smile and wave at the person behind us in line all day long, but we never impact them with kindness unless we act in a way that changes their circumstance.

In the situation you described above where you saw someone's circumstance, did you act? Explain.

Stressful situations tend to bring our focus inward. Pursuing acts of kindness helps us keep our focus outward. A simple act of kindness has a profound effect on those around us as well as on our own state of mind.

Splash of Prayer

Pray today that God reveals opportunities for you to take the initiative to show kindness. Then act!

Visible Faithfulness

 ## Daily Drop

Therefore, my dear brothers, be steadfast, immovable, always excelling in the Lord's work, knowing that your labor in the Lord is not in vain.

—1 CORINTHIANS 15:58 HCSB

It is hard to believe, in a time when black and white is a novelty, that some people do not dream in color. I wonder if the invention of Technicolor skewed the averages on that. The world may never know.

Joseph had some experience with dreams. Exposing his dreams to his family eventually led him to be a slave in prison. Despite his circumstance, Joseph remained steadfast in his faithfulness to God. He served well and lived daily with immovable integrity. Joseph's faithful lifestyle kept him steady while waiting for his dreams to become a reality.

Thinking back over Joseph's experiences thus far, what are some key points of faithfulness you can identify?

Joseph's fellow prisoners also had dreams. They were visibly shaken because they had no one to interpret them. Let's travel a little further with Joseph in this conversation.

Read Genesis 40:7–13.

Faithfulness is a fruit of the Spirit. Ephesians 5:18 instructs us to be "filled by the Spirit." Galatians 5:16 tells us we are to "walk by the Spirit," and a few verses later Paul explains that the fruit of the Spirit freely flows from us as we walk in Him.

When a tree bears fruit, the tree has something to show. If it is an apple tree, then there are visible apples. If a lemon tree, visible lemons. In the same manner, when a Christian bears fruit, there must be something to show for it. There must be visible representations of that fruit.

Are you bearing spiritual fruit? What is the visible representation of each fruit you are bearing?

In this section of the story, we see very visible representations of faithfulness in Joseph's actions. First, Joseph was faithful to bear witness. He was quick to point out that interpreting dreams was God's business, not his. If he had not made that statement, the men could have easily given the credit for what was about to happen to him. Joseph made sure the glory went to God alone.

We too can show faithfulness by giving God the glory in every part of our lives. James tells us that "every good and perfect gift is from above, and comes down from the Father" (James 1:17). We do well to audibly give Him the glory for it all as we fulfill our commission to be ambassadors for Christ.

What was the last blessing you audibly gave God the glory for?

Second, Joseph continued in faithful service by doing the Lord's work as he gave the interpretation of the dream. By stating up front that God was the interpreter, Joseph made it clear that he was simply a mouthpiece sharing what God revealed to him.

We experience God every day. He speaks to us through His Word, through sermons, through songs, through friends, sometimes even through enemies, and He speaks to us in the stillness of our quiet time. The Lord works in and through our lives every day. It is our responsibility as Christians to share what He reveals to us, what we learn from the experiences He allows in our lives, and the comfort we receive from Him. We bring glory and honor to our Lord and Savior by sharing with others the wisdom He reveals to us.

What was the last thing the Lord revealed to you? Who have you shared it with?

Last, Joseph showed his faithfulness by being faithful. Let me explain. We love God because He first loved us. We forgive others because Christ forgave us and gave His very life to save us. And we are faithful because the Lord was first faithful to us. There is nothing good about us in and of ourselves. We are all fatally guilty of sin, unrighteous. We are unfaithful by nature. It is only through the blood of Christ that we are washed whiter than snow. It is only through the blood at the cross and the power of the Spirit within us that we can be seen by the Father as His children, co-heirs with Christ. Faithful. As Donna Gaines so beautifully described it, we are to be "accurate representations"[1] of Christ.

How accurate is your representation of Christ? What is God leading you to do today to improve your accuracy?

When we achieve faithful witness, faithful work, and consistent faithfulness, our representation of Christ becomes more accurate, and, like Joseph, our labors will not be in vain.

 ## Splash of Prayer

Ask the Lord to reveal to you today an area where you have opportunity to be a more "accurate representation" of Christ.

Embrace the Wait

Daily Drop

You are my hiding place; You shall preserve me from trouble; You shall surround me with songs of deliverance.

—PSALM 32:7

God's Word is full of stories of deliverance. God delivered Noah and his family from a worldwide flood. God will no doubt deliver Joseph from captivity in His perfect timing. Is there any doubt God will deliver us from our difficulty in His perfect timing as well?

Read Psalm 18:2; 40:17; 61:3; 144:2.

What are the names of God listed in these verses in your version of God's Word?

How often do you claim God as each of these in your life?

Claiming and praying the names of God is a powerful weapon as we strive to stay Christlike in the midst of our trouble. To deliver means to set free. In Matthew 6:13, Jesus instructs us to pray for God to deliver us from evil.

During the praise of Psalm 32, David tells us God will surround us with songs of deliverance, songs of being set free. David claims God as his hiding place, and he is confident that God will preserve him from his trouble.

Preserve does not mean remove. Preserve means to keep safe from harm or destruction. The HCSB uses the word protect here. To protect is to defend, shield, and shelter. Neither translation implies that David is immediately removed from his trouble. The psalm does promise a hiding place and protection while he embraces the wait, listening to sweet songs promising deliverance. He has confidence that deliverance will come in God's timing.

When we left Joseph, he was interpreting the cupbearer's dream while he embraced his own wait. Although Joseph was in prison, he had indeed felt the protecting hand of God. Let's pick up there now.

Read Genesis 40:12–15.

Here, for the first time after all these years, we see Joseph pleading his case. In the HCSB translation he plainly stated, "show kindness" and "get me out of this prison." What sparked this sudden urge to change his circumstance? Did the interpretation of dreams remind Joseph of his own dreams years before? Perhaps he remembered that God had revealed to him he would one day rule over his family. How could that ever happen from prison? Joseph was perhaps thinking that it was time to move on with the fulfillment of his own dreams.

When the baker heard the favorable interpretation of the cupbearer's dream, he likely expected a similar interpretation for his own dream. Let's continue.

Read Genesis 40:16–19.

Hmmm. I am guessing this was not exactly the interpretation the baker had hoped for. Scripture doesn't reveal how either man reacted to Joseph's interpretation, but we do see what followed.

Read Genesis 40:20–41:1.

Three days later, Pharaoh's birthday was an eventful day for both the cupbearer and the baker. Joseph's interpretations of their dreams came to pass just as he had said. Verse 23 is devastating news for Joseph. In the hustle and bustle of the birthday festivities and the elation of being out of prison, the cupbearer forgot about Joseph. And he did so for quite some time. I included verse 41:1 so you can see the amount of time that passed. "Two years later . . ." The forgetfulness of the cupbearer resulted in two more years of imprisonment for Joseph.

Again we are left with a great void in details over a two-year span of time. Surely Joseph knew the baker and the cupbearer had been released from prison. He had most likely heard of the demise of the baker. Perhaps he even heard of the cupbearer proudly filling his station again. And he waited. And he waited. And he waited. I wonder how long it took for Joseph to realize he had been forgotten.

Do you feel you are in a season of waiting today? Explain.

In times when God is silent, it would be very easy to think God has forgotten you. That is simply never the case. When God says wait, He has His divine reasons that are ultimately for your good and His glory. Let's look at a few verses around embracing the wait.

> Wait on the Lord; be of good courage, And He shall strengthen your heart; Wait, I say, on the Lord!
>
> —PSALM 27:14

> Wait on the Lord , And keep His way, And He shall exalt you to inherit the land; when the wicked are cut off, you shall see it.
>
> —PSALM 37:34

> Be still, and know that I am God; I will be exalted among the nations, I will be exalted in the earth!
>
> —PSALM 46:10

> But those who wait on the Lord Shall renew their strength; They shall mount up with wings like eagles, They shall run and not be weary, They shall walk and not faint.
>
> —ISAIAH 40:31

> The Lord is good to those who wait for Him, To the soul who seeks Him. It is good that one should hope and wait quietly for the salvation of the Lord.
>
> —LAMENTATIONS 3:25–26

Do any of these verses give you specific comfort in your current situation? Explain.

Waiting is never easy, but when we embrace it with faith, it will bring glory to God the Father. Jesus taught us to pray, "Thy will be done," and more times than not, God's timing does not line up with ours.

Joseph knew God's prophetic promises to him and his family. The children of Abraham, Isaac, and Jacob were promised to be a great nation. Joseph was promised that he would rule over his family. Remembering God's promises no doubt enabled Joseph to embrace the wait for God's perfect timing of his deliverance. In the interim, God would preserve him.

Likewise, God preserves us from our trouble. He surrounds us with songs of the promise of His deliverance. He is our hiding place. Embrace the wait in His capable care.

 ## Splash of Prayer

Ask God to show you how He has preserved you in the past. Thank Him. Then trust Him for preservation in the future.

LESSON

16

Give God Glory

To God our Savior, Who alone is wise, Be glory and majesty, Dominion and power, Both now and forever. Amen.

—JUDE 25

The Weather Channel called Hurricane Florence a "slow-moving disaster." Once a category 4 hurricane, she hit the coast of the Carolinas at only a category 2, then quickly diminished to a tropical storm. So why the disaster? She stalled just off the coast and hovered there, dumping feet of rain on an already saturated area.

Likewise, some storms of life, although not as strong as they could be, hover and greatly outstay their welcome. Thirteen years into his captivity, Joseph must have felt as though his storm clouds would never clear. He may not yet have recognized that freedom was very close for him.

Read Genesis 41:1–16.

Joseph's story has been a story of dreams. It all started with two dreams, and then we saw two more dreams in the middle. Now, as we near the end, we

70

find two final dreams that will ultimately solidify Joseph's destiny. While Pharaoh struggled with the meaning of his dreams, the cupbearer suddenly regained his memory and remembered Joseph!

Joseph had remained steadfast and strong for the Lord, and now he was finally being remembered. Rest assured, God had never forgotten Joseph. God jostled the cupbearer's memory at the exact time Joseph needed to be remembered in order to fulfill his destiny.

Do you feel that your situation is forgotten today? How does this turn in the story encourage you?

Joseph's head must have been spinning as he made a hasty trip from the dungeon into the presence of Pharaoh. He had spent years in the dungeon. Yes, Joseph had embraced the wait and made the best of it, knowing God was with him, but he had been in prison, nevertheless. It speaks a bit to his living conditions that he had to be cleaned up before going before the ruler of Egypt.

Pharaoh wasted no time. He got straight to the point when he told Joseph that he had a dream and none could interpret it. "But I have heard that when you hear about a dream you can interpret it" (Genesis 41:16 NLT).

Joseph was center stage in the most important meeting of his life thus far. His future was hanging in the balance. Some might think to take matters into their own hands by claiming abilities and making promises in order to be free from imprisonment. Joseph made one of the most brave and powerful statements, in my opinion, of his entire journey.

> **"It is beyond my power to do this."**
>
> —GENESIS 41:16 NLT

Standing before the ruler of a nation, Joseph said, "I cannot do this." Joseph stripped himself of any glory or power to control the outcome of this meeting. In the presence of Pharaoh, he relinquished full control to the King of Glory.

Describe a time when you felt powerless and incapable of doing what was being asked of you.

Thankfully, Joseph's story doesn't end with "I cannot" and neither does yours. Don't you love a good, "But God . . ."?

> **"But God can tell you what it means and set you at ease."**
>
> —GENESIS 41:16 NLT

Joseph gave God all the glory. He claimed not one thing for himself. It would do us all a world of good to live out the statement, "It is beyond my power to . . ., but God can . . ."

Oh, yes! God can interpret dreams. God can calm our fears. God can heal our wounds. God can move our mountains. And God can deliver us from our difficulties. Believe it! God can! God will! God does! He is able! Give Him all the glory for everything in your life.

Complete the following statements.

It is beyond my power to _____

But God can _____

Like Joseph, we would do well to recognize that God can do what we cannot. Allow God to empower your situation. Remember that when we are weak, that's when He uses His strength. Give Him control and watch the miracles unfold in your life as you grow spiritually through your circumstances.

Natalie Grant is one of my favorite Christian singers. She posted the following on social media after she had undergone a surgery. I hope these powerful words encourage you as much as they do me.

> I'm beyond grateful for the health and healing that's happening in my soul . . . learning to seek His face, before I seek His hand. Learning to declare His goodness regardless of my outcome. Recognizing once again that it's not just what He does for me but WHO HE IS. He is the miracle. He is the prize. Jesus more than anything. What is your need today? Ask Him for the miracle. He invites us to do so. But don't have your heart and mind so set on the end of your circumstance that you miss what He wants to do in the middle of your circumstance. Some of you are in the fight of your life and don't know if you can take another step. I promise what you think may destroy you, can be what delivers you—turning you into a warrior with a fire nothing and no one can extinguish. All that you need, He's already done. Jesus more than anything.[1]

 ## Splash of Prayer

Look up, child of God. Do you see Jesus watching over you? Reach for Him with all that is within you. You cannot do this . . . but God can.

LESSON

17

Let Your Light Shine

 Daily Drop

"Let your light so shine before men, that they may see your good works and glorify your Father in heaven."

—MATTHEW 5:16

Winter can feel long and dreary. The sun doesn't show its face very often, and the nights are long and cold. Some areas of the country are buried in snow for months. Then finally, the sun breaks through the clouds. That first ray of sunshine is so bright we have to squint to see. The darkness of winter is over, and the warm sunshine of spring overcomes the cold. We cannot help but turn our faces up to the heavens and soak it all in.

We might imagine Joseph had a similar feeling as his years of slavery began to fall behind him. Now we see that ray of light breaking through as God's deliverance shone on Joseph.

Read Genesis 41:17–38.

Joseph not only communicated the interpretation of the dreams but also gave exact instructions regarding what had to be done to save Egypt from the years of famine. God gave both the warning and the solution.

74

Why was God so concerned with saving Egypt from a famine?

Remember, Jacob, renamed Israel by God, was still alive. The nation of Israel was a fledgling family. One family alone in a foreign land could not survive a famine of this magnitude. Joseph's deliverance was right on time to position him to fulfill God's plan. He was to deliver God's message to Pharaoh in order to save Egypt—and Israel. Joseph may not have yet realized his full part in this plan, but he was obedient, fully trusting God's direction.

Your God-given destiny and mine might not save a nation. But all the same, it is part of God's master plan. Everything in our lives is there for a reason. God is in control. He has either allowed your circumstance or orchestrated it in order to fulfill His purpose for you. If you are encountering a difficulty, then you can rest assured that God is working out something in and through you. He is constantly molding you into the Christian He wants you to be. You are here, in this situation, for such a time as this.

What is God working out in you?

If you don't know, what are some of the lessons you have learned through trials? Do they point to a grander purpose?

The truth is, God's purpose for your difficulty may never be completely clear to you. But know that it will be completed. It is not God's intention that we understand everything. God confirms this in His Word.

For as the heavens are higher than the earth, so are My ways higher than your ways, and My thoughts than your thoughts.

—ISAIAH 55:9

God's ways are high, often out of the reach of our carnal minds. But as we dive into His Word, He will guide us to fulfill His purpose.

Your word is a lamp to my feet and a light to my path.

—PSALM 119:105

You need only a lamp or a light when it's dark and you cannot see. In true darkness, a flashlight illuminates only a few feet in front of you. You can see the next step or two but not the full journey. I find great comfort in the fact that God's Word lights the path in front of me. He allows me to see just far enough to move forward in faith. The faith required to walk—and to make spiritual progress—in the dark requires surrender and obedience. He knows the way. I don't have to. I just need to trust Him and follow His light.

Is there an area where you feel as if you can see only a few feet in front of you? Describe. How can trust, surrender, and obedience help you?

Back to Joseph. His suggestions were "well received" (Genesis 41:37 NLT). Why? Because he was "so obviously filled with the Spirit of God" (verse 38). Joseph radiated the very Spirit that had been growing stronger and stronger within him throughout his captivity.

This side of the cross, every believer is Spirit-filled. The Holy Spirit comes to live within us at the moment of salvation. Our challenge is not to be filled but rather to allow the Spirit within us to radiate out. The Light within us can light the path for others when we allow that to happen. Please ponder these questions with me for a few moments.

When have you been recognized as "so obviously filled with the Spirit"?

How are you currently radiating the Spirit of God?

If we continually rely on God, we will become more and more Christlike, and the Spirit will freely radiate from us. People will notice something different. Even the pagan Pharaoh recognized the Spirit of the one true God when he was face-to-face with Him.

On the contrary, if we begin to rely on ourselves, the Spirit is quenched. If we are in control, the Lord is not. Whether we understand our purpose clearly, or it has not yet been revealed, it is our duty as Christians to surrender daily to the Lord. When we are in a state of obedience, we have no control. He has full control. This allows the Spirit, who has filled us, to radiate freely from within us. We were made to glorify God by letting our light shine! Shine bright, sister!

 ## Splash of Prayer

Thank the Lord today for His light that leads the way. Allow the Spirit to shine from within you.

LESSON 18

God Will Supply

 ## Daily Drop

And my God shall supply all your need according to His riches in glory by Christ Jesus.

—PHILIPPIANS 4:19

Why is it that super smart kids always seem to be so skinny? Their small stature plus their intelligence set them up as prime targets to be picked on as children. Bill Gates advises, "Be nice to nerds. Chances are you'll end up working for one."[1] Often that tends to be true. These intelligent children grow up to be mature professionals who climb the ladder to success at lightning speed.

Joseph was a seventeen-year-old boy when he was sold into slavery. He was mistreated, falsely accused, imprisoned, and forgotten. In God's perfect timing, Joseph was remembered, brought before Pharaoh, and empowered by God to interpret Pharaoh's dreams. God also gave Pharaoh, through Joseph, a plan to survive the devastation to come. Let's see how the next scene unfolded.

Read Genesis 41:37–46.

At thirty years of age, Joseph was a mature, God-honoring, God-fearing man. With his life fully submerged in his faith in God's love and care, he was recognized for his intelligence and, most importantly, his close relationship with God. I wonder how Potiphar and the jailers felt as they saw this slave boy rise to ruler.

Who was Joseph given charge over?

What items did Pharaoh give Joseph?

I suspect that Joseph's head was once again spinning as these events unfolded. He knew God's promises to his forefathers, and he knew God's promises through his dreams. But could he have ever imagined that God would fulfill those promises in this magnificent way?

Recall a time when your head was spinning because of a magnificent work of God on your behalf. Describe.

We see in these verses some very significant items Joseph was given. Let's look a little closer.

First, Joseph was given Pharaoh's signet ring from his own hand. This was no ordinary ring. It was engraved with the symbol of Pharaoh's house. The signet ring allowed Joseph the full authority of Pharaoh to carry out God's plan. With this ring, Joseph had authority over all the land of Egypt.

Next we see Joseph's prison clothes replaced by fine linen attire accessorized by a chain of gold. Now Joseph looked the part. Where Joseph's coat of many colors had once draped, now the garments of a king, representing the fate of a nation, rested squarely on his shoulders.

Joseph was also given royal transportation. He rode in the second chariot behind Pharaoh. Shouts of "Bow the knee!" were called to the crowds. As the nation of Egypt bowed before Joseph, he could surely see the fulfillment of his prophetic dreams close behind. His family would soon bow the knee before him as well, just as God had revealed in his dreams thirteen long years before.

Finally, Joseph was given a wife. This was no ordinary woman. Asenath was the daughter of a priest of the sun god, Ra. Asenath, a Gentile, would be the mother of two tribes of Israel. It is surely evident by the faith and heritage of her boys that Asenath must have forsaken the gods of her father and believed in the one true God of Abraham, Isaac, Jacob, and Joseph. In this picture of Joseph's transformation from slave to ruler we see authority, responsibility, and salvation. As God works out your transformation, what do you see?

What has God given you to fulfill your destiny?

What does it represent?

We have just examined what God provided at this step in Joseph's journey. We must keep in mind that God had been providing for Joseph for the entire thirteen years he was in prison. God had been carefully grooming Joseph for this day, and in response, Joseph had submerged himself in God's promise, as seen in his willingness to give Him all the glory all along the way.

I recognize that even though Joseph has been freed, you may not yet be free from your situation. I hope you find comfort in the fact that God was supplying what Joseph needed every step of the way. Today is necessary to accomplish tomorrow. As we press on, growing toward our destiny, God will provide exactly what we need every step of the way. That is His promise.

 ## Splash of Prayer

Ask God to reveal His divine provision for you. Then thank Him.

LESSON

19

Take Time to Look Back

Daily Drop

"With men this is impossible, but with God all things are possible."
— MATTHEW 19:26

Things often look a lot clearer in our rearview mirror. As we are traveling through our struggles, life is often foggy and hard to traverse. But when the struggle subsides, when the fog clears, that's when we can often see God's hand on the entire journey.

For Joseph, the tide had turned. He and his wife had two sons. Just as God had revealed to Joseph, there were seven years of bumper crops. Joseph followed God's plan and filled the storehouses, preparing for the famine to come.

The famine years began, not only in Egypt but also in the surrounding countries. People from all around came to buy grain from Joseph. Jacob, Joseph's father, heard there was grain in Egypt and sent his sons to buy the food they needed to keep them alive.

Joseph immediately recognized his brothers when they came, but they didn't recognize him. Genesis 42–44 tells the story of how Joseph interacted with his brothers. Finally, in Genesis 45, Joseph revealed his identity and his destiny.

Read Genesis 45:1–8.

We see Joseph's raw emotion here as he revealed his identity to his brothers. The New Living Translation says that the brothers were "stunned" to see Joseph standing in front of them. I bet! The last time they'd seen him, he was a scrawny teenage boy being sold into a life of slavery. Now here he stood, the most powerful man in Egypt other than Pharaoh himself. I would imagine it was the grip of sheer fear that rendered them speechless. But Joseph had something to say. Did he say I told you so? Did he say vengeance is mine? No. That wasn't who Joseph was. Joseph began to explain how God had orchestrated the entire journey. What a revelation that must have been. You can almost hear the pieces of the puzzle clicking together.

Joseph was aware that the hand of God had been working around him all those years. He could have spent those years angry and upset about his circumstances, but that would not have fulfilled his destiny. Joseph trusted God through the entire experience. As a result, he was able to trace God's plan through all that happened. Joseph understood that his trials had prepared him for this very task.

As our difficulties resolve, it is helpful to look back and recognize God's plan and His loving hand guiding us. We can "backward engineer" our journey to find God's fingerprints along the way.

Joseph knew that God, not his brothers, had sent him to Egypt. Let's take a moment to backward engineer Joseph's experience and see God's hand on him through the rearview mirror.

- Joseph saved many from the famine. He couldn't have done that, if he hadn't been Pharaoh's advisor.

- He became Pharaoh's advisor because he interpreted Pharaoh's dreams.

- He was brought to interpret Pharaoh's dreams because the cupbearer remembered Him.

- The cupbearer remembered him because Joseph had interpreted his dream.

- Joseph was available to interpret the cupbearer's dream because he was in prison.

- Joseph was in prison because he was falsely accused by Potiphar's wife.

- Joseph was in Potiphar's house with his wife because he was his slave.

- Joseph was a slave because his brothers had sold him.

- His brothers sold him because he dreamed he would rule over them; also, they were jealous of their father's preference for this younger son, shown by the colorful coat he had been given.

We have come full circle. The dream that started it all had become reality. God allowed everything to happen as it did because He knew the outcome. God knew every step along the way brought Joseph a step closer to his destiny.

What circumstance can you backward engineer and see God's plan?

Give it a try.

Many accounts in the Bible can be backward engineered to show God's master plan. I dare say there are many accounts in our own lives in which, if we just look for God's hand, we can see His purpose.

For Joseph, God meant it for good (Genesis 50:20).

For Esther, it was for such a time as this (Esther 4:14).

For Jesus, it was because God so loved the world (John 3:16).

For those of us who love God, all things work together for good (Romans 8:28).

We could go on and on with examples of how God works in mysterious ways to accomplish His perfect plan for mankind. We, my friend, are blessed to be a part of that amazing plan!

Our God is big, and He desires to be big in and through our lives—in the good times and the bad. He is a mountain-moving, wind-ruling, water-parting Savior. If He doesn't move your mountain, then it is His will that you climb it. If He doesn't calm your storm, then it's His intent that you weather it. And if He doesn't part the water before you, my friend, He intends for you to swim!

I encourage you today to embrace your journey. Dive into Scripture. Trust in God and follow His guidance all the way to your destiny.

Splash of Prayer

Thank God today for every one of His fingerprints you can see on your life. Then thank Him for those fingerprints that are so delicate you can't see them.

Confident Hope

Daily Drop

I pray that God, the source of hope, will fill you completely with joy and peace because you trust in him. Then you will overflow with confident hope through the power of the Holy Spirit.

—ROMANS 15:13 NLT

Joseph led an incredible life. Today it would be billed as a "riches-to-rags-to-riches" story. He was the favored son of a patriarch. Then the moment God made him realize he was destined for even greater things, he found himself in a pit, sold as a slave, and then falsely accused and in prison. Living under the protection of his father, Joseph would have never learned the things he needed to know in order to fulfill God's plan for him.

Joseph was tasked with the largest food drive on record. The planning and management skills required were at CEO levels. He needed unbending integrity and compassionate kindness. His faith had to be steadfast and his trust in God unyielding. His seventeen-year-old-boy résumé simply did not fit the bill. Joseph needed training, and God provided. By the time thirty-year-old Joseph was put in charge of Egypt, God had assembled quite the résumé for him. At his first post, Joseph managed Potiphar's household well, and he prospered. His faith was tested, and his integrity was proven. His second assignment, this time in prison, boosted his résumé considerably more. There he was responsible for all the prisoners, and he managed the prison well. His trust in God was put to the test, and once again he passed with flying colors. He served God by serving others with compassion and kindness. God was growing Joseph's skills to the level needed to fulfill his ultimate assignment, the deliverance of Egypt and Israel from famine.

Life is frequently a struggle. We think we have our path figured out. Then we discover another challenge, another detour, another struggle. Knowing Joseph's story gives me courage and strength to press on. Joseph's story, like so many others in the Bible, gives us hope because we have assurance God will never leave us in the middle of our struggle. He has a purpose to fulfill through us, and He will lead us to it, all along the way teaching us what we need to know when we get there.

How does Joseph's story give you hope?

What is God teaching you right now that is strengthening your spiritual résumé?

Let's move forward to the end of Joseph's story. Joseph sent his brothers back to Canaan to bring his father and the entire family back to Egypt. There they would have plenty of food to make it through the remaining years of the famine.

Please read Genesis 46:1–7.

God moved the children of Israel from Canaan to Egypt, but not without a promise that they would return someday and inherit the land God had given their forefathers. God spoke to Jacob in a vision, assuring him that moving to Egypt was the right thing to do. The total number of Jacob's direct descendants who moved to Egypt, not including his daughters-in-law, was sixty-six. Joseph and his family, of course, were already there.

Jacob was one hundred and thirty years old when he and his family, with their flocks and herds, traveled to Goshen, where they lived and multiplied. He lived seventeen more years before his health failed him.

Please read Genesis 48:1–22.

Joseph's two sons would receive the same inheritance as each of Jacob's sons. Jacob blessed his other eleven sons as well. Then, there in the land of Egypt, Jacob breathed his last as God had told him he would. Joseph and his brothers buried their father in the land of Canaan as Joseph had promised him they would.

Once Jacob had passed, Joseph's brothers were sure that Joseph would take revenge on them. They didn't understand the maturity and wisdom Joseph possessed. They didn't understand that this had all been a part of God's master plan.

Please read Genesis 50:14–25.

Joseph's last bit of wisdom for us is that we are not to judge. Judgment and punishment belong to the Lord alone. We are to love and forgive. And that is just what Joseph did.

The Lord is the source of our hope. He cannot fill us with joy and peace if we are willingly withholding love and forgiveness. When we rid ourselves of unforgiveness, the Holy Spirit is free to do His work in us. He doesn't supply just fragile hope. He fills our spirit to the point of overflowing with confident hope.

Whom do you need to forgive today?

I encourage you to unleash the Spirit within you by extending love and forgiveness where it's needed. Then get ready to overflow with confident hope!

Joseph's family continued to live in the land of Egypt, and Joseph took care of them. Joseph died at the ripe old age of one hundred and ten. He died with the assurance that God would bring the children of Israel out of Egypt and back into the promised land of Canaan in His time. And God did just that. As promised, the children of Israel took Joseph's bones with them when they exited Egypt. That's another wonderful story for another day!

I have so enjoyed studying Joseph's journey with you. It is my prayer for you that your life be filled with confident hope. I pray you see God's fingerprints all over every day you live. When a new journey lies before you, dive into Scripture! God will provide everything you need to fulfill His plan for you. Stand strong in your battles. Radiate Christlikeness in all circumstances. In God's time, you will be victorious, and our Lord will receive all the praise and honor and glory as you share your story of His deliverance with those He puts in your path. It is your destiny!

 ## Splash of Prayer

Thank God today for the journey He has placed you on. Ask Him for guidance that will allow you, like Joseph, to grow spiritually and fulfill the destiny He has in store for you.

Grace to you and peace from God our Father
and the Lord Jesus Christ.

—EPHESIANS 1:2

About the Author

Lynn Wise is an IT professional with a passion for Women's Ministry. She is a Bible teacher, author of four Bible studies, and an active participant in women's ministry in her local church.

She wrote and taught her first Bible study based on Psalm 24 in 2014. Since then she has been writing and teaching Bible studies as the Lord leads. Her primary motivation is to help women draw closer to one another and closer to Christ as they study and apply God's Word to their everyday lives.

Lynn lives in New Albany, Mississippi, with her dog, Toby. She is a member of Hillcrest Baptist Church, also in New Albany. Her daughter, Jessica, and son-in-law, Rob, live nearby. They have blessed her with two beautiful grandchildren, Fisher and Olivia Hart, who affectionately know her as "BumBum."

Notes

Preface

1. *Quotefancy*, s.v. "Stephen R. Covey," accessed August 26, 2019, http://www. quotefancy.com.

Lesson 1

1. Mark Batterson. *In a Pit with a Lion on a Snowy Day* (New York: Multnomah, 2006), iBooks, chap. 1.

Lesson 5

1. *The Daily Walk Bible* (Wheaton, IL: Tyndale House Publishers, Inc., 1997), 50.

Lesson 8

1. *Goodreads*, s.v. "John Lyly > Quotes," accessed August 26, 2019, https://www. goodreads.com/author/quotes/139084.John_Lyly.

2. Charles Marshall. "Where is the man who will do the right thing, no matter what the cost?" *Charles Marshall, Humorous Motivational Speaker* (blog), July 31, 2012, http://charlesmarshall.net/where-is-the-man-who-will-do-the-right-thing-no-matter-what-the-cost/.

3. Henry David Thoreau, *AZ Quotes*, s.v. "Idle Hands Quotes," accessed August 26, 2019, https://www.azquotes.com/quotes/topics/idle-hands.html.

4. Voddie Baucham, Jr. *Family Conference* (sermon, Hillcrest Baptist Church, New Albany, MS, January 20, 2018).

5. *Daily Inspirational Quotes,* accessed August 28, 2019, https://www. dailyinspirationalquotes.in/2012/08/trust-takes-years-to-build-seconds-to-break-and-wisdom-quotes/.

Lesson 9

1. *Forrest Gump*, directed by Robert Zemickis (Hollywood, CA: Paramount Pictures, 1994).

Lesson 10

1. Harry Champion, "I'm Henry VIII, I Am," *Herman's Hermits Lyrics*, accessed August 26, 2019, https://www.azlyrics.com/lyrics/hermanshermits/imhenryviiiiam.html.

2. Mark Batterson. *In a Pit with a Lion on a Snowy Day* (New York: Multnomah, 2006), iBooks, chap. 7.

3. Charles H. Spurgeon. "The Jeer of Sarcasm, and the Retort of Piety" (sermon no. 321, New Park Street Pulpit, Vol. 6, April 8, 1860), accessed August 28, 2019, https://www.spurgeon.org/resource-library/sermons/the-jeer-of-sarcasm-and-the-retort-of-piety#flipbook/.

Lesson 11

1. Dale Schiller, friend and confidant, 2018.

2. *BrainyQuote*, s.v. "Henry Ford Quotes," accessed August 26, 2019, https://www.brainyquote.com/authors/henry-ford-quotes.

Lesson 12

1. *BrainQuote*, s.v. "Albert Einstein Quotes," accessed August 26, 2019, https://www.brainyquote.com/authors/albert-einstein-quotes.

2. Judy Huddleston, friend and confidant, 2016.

3. Warren W. Wiersbe. *The Wiersbe Bible Commentary NT*, 2nd Ed. (Colorado Springs, CO: David C. Cook, 2007), 654.

Lesson 13

1. *BrainyQuote*, s.v. Peter Drucker, accessed March 9, 2019, https://www. brainyquote.com /authors/peter-drucker-quotes

Lesson 14

1. Donna Gaines, "Choose Wisely, Live Fully" (lecture, First Baptist Church, Baldwyn, MS, November 2, 2017).

Lesson 16

1. Natalie Grant's Facebook page, April 11, 2018, https://www.facebook.com/ pg/nataliegrantmusic/posts/

Lesson 18

1. Bill Gates, "Bill Gates speech: 14 rules your kids did not and will not learn in school" (Facebook post), September 12, 2010, https://www.facebook.com/ notes/tea-talk-and-gossip/bill-gates-speech-14-rules-your-kids-did-not-and-will-not-learn-in-school/152862328071768/.

Made in the
USA
Columbia, SC

78656911R00057